CELEBRATING THE FAMILY NAME OF HUGHES

Celebrating the Family Name of Hughes

Walter the Educator

Silent King Books
a WhichHead Entertainment Imprint

Copyright © 2024 by Walter the Educator

All rights reserved. No part of this book may be reproduced in any manner whatsoever without written permission except in the case of brief quotations embodied in critical articles and reviews.

First Printing, 2024

Disclaimer

This book is a literary work; the story is not about specific persons, locations, situations, and/or circumstances unless mentioned in a historical context. Any resemblance to real persons, locations, situations, and/or circumstances is coincidental. This book is for entertainment and informational purposes only. The author and publisher offer this information without warranties expressed or implied. No matter the grounds, neither the author nor the publisher will be accountable for any losses, injuries, or other damages caused by the reader's use of this book. The use of this book acknowledges an understanding and acceptance of this disclaimer.

Celebrating the Family Name of Hughes is a memory book that belongs to the Celebrating Family Name Book Series by Walter the Educator. Collect them all and more books at WaltertheEducator.com

USE THE EXTRA SPACE TO DOCUMENT YOUR FAMILY MEMORIES THROUGHOUT THE YEARS

HUGHES

In the quiet of the night, when the world is still,

Celebrating the Family Name of

Hughes

The name Hughes echoes from valley to hill.

It's a name like the wind, both gentle and strong,

A melody ancient, a soul's lasting song.

Hughes, a name carved in the heart of the earth,

Born of endurance, and crafted in worth.

It's more than just letters, more than a sound—

It's the pulse of the ages, deep and profound.

Like the stars in the heavens, Hughes shines bright,

Guiding its kin through the darkest of night.

It's a name that whispers of courage untold,

Of ancestors whose hearts were both daring and bold.

From lands far and wide, where the rivers run free,

The Hughes name is rooted in history's sea.

It flows through the fields, where hard work was sown,

And in every Hughes heart, its legacy is known.

Celebrating the Family Name of

Hughes

There's a wisdom in Hughes, passed down like a flame,

A light that's unwavering, always the same.

It carries the stories of battles long fought,

Of struggles endured, of dreams finely wrought.

The Hughes family knows how to weather the storm,

To stand in the rain, to keep their hearts warm.

With hands that have built and minds that create,

They've mastered the art of bending fate.

In the quiet moments when the world turns slow,

The name Hughes is a river with a steady flow.

It moves with intention, with purpose and grace,

Leaving behind a trail time can't erase.

Hughes is the mountain that stands ever tall,

A beacon of strength through summer and fall.

It reaches the heavens, yet roots deep in the ground,

Celebrating the Family Name of

Hughes

A family whose legacy knows no bound.

They are dreamers and doers, with fire in their soul,

With hearts that are humble, but minds that are whole.

Each generation brings forth something new,

Yet honors the past in all that they do.

There's poetry in Hughes, in the way that they live,

A rhythm of kindness, of love they give.

It's a name that speaks not with boast or with pride,

But with quiet assurance and wisdom inside.

ABOUT THE CREATOR

Walter the Educator is one of the pseudonyms for Walter Anderson. Formally educated in Chemistry, Business, and Education, he is an educator, an author, a diverse entrepreneur, and he is the son of a disabled war veteran. "Walter the Educator" shares his time between educating and creating. He holds interests and owns several creative projects that entertain, enlighten, enhance, and educate, hoping to inspire and motivate you. Follow, find new works, and stay up to date with Walter the Educator™

at WaltertheEducator.com

www.ingramcontent.com/pod-product-compliance
Lightning Source LLC
LaVergne TN
LVHW010622070526
838199LV00063BA/5233